An op

BRISTOL

Written by
FLORENCE FILOSE

CONTRIBUTORS

Florence Filose is a writer and editor born and raised in the West Country, who moved to London in her twenties before remembering all the reasons that Bristol is better. She now lives and works back in Bristol, where she splits her time between sampling local ciders and pushing her bike up hills.

Hoxton Mini Press is a small indie publisher based in east London. We make books about London (and beyond) with a dedication to lovely, sustainable production and brilliant photography. When we started the company, people told us 'print was dead'; we wanted to prove them wrong. Books are no longer about information but objects in their own right: things to collect and own and inspire. We are an environmentally conscious publisher, committed to offsetting our carbon footprint. This book, for instance, is 100 per cent carbon compensated, with offset purchased from Stand for Trees.

INFORMATION IS DEAD. LONG LIVE OPINION.

Why bother with a guidebook? Everything you need to know is online.

Not true! While you can find endless information on the internet, it's not so easy to find the RIGHT information. This, here in your hands, is opinionated, reliable, local information, reduced like a fine sauce.

We are a small indie publisher in Hackney and this is the latest book in our series of unashamedly pithy guides to places that we really rate. How dare we write about Bristol from Hackney? Well, one of our finest editors, Florence, left us to go (back) to Bristol because she thought it so much better than London. So we asked her to tell us what was so excellent, and here is her answer. We strongly suggest you go with the Flo.

(This page) Colston Street, city centre
(Opposite) The Bristol Loaf (no.6)

(This page) The Matthew (no.36)
(Opposite) Artist Residence Bristol (no.59)

THE BRISTOL BUZZ

Welcome to Bristol. Home to the UK's longest independent shopping street, over 400 green spaces, a food scene built on the words 'locally sourced' and more street art than you can shake a spray can at, this colourful, cultural, community-minded city has a history dating back to Anglo-Saxon times and a reputation for creative free thinking delivered with West Country wit.

It was the first British city to be named a European Green Capital, as well as the UK's first 'cycling city', thanks to its commitment to sustainable travel (trust me, you do have to be pretty committed to tackle its many hills by bike). There's a thriving urban culture here, with a proliferation of artists, students, performers and activists lighting up Bristol's venues and protesting on its streets. But there's also sprawling countryside wrapped snugly around the city, so a view from any of its apexes stretches for miles. And if living by water has been proven to make you happier, then Bristolians' renowned cheerfulness might be attributed to its bustling docks and network of rivers and canals that make waterbus one of the best ways to take a tour.

Perhaps all this makes you think it's hard to go wrong with a weekend in Bristol? Not quite. There are still plenty of chain restaurants, overpriced hotels and uninspiring tourist outlets to lead you astray. We won't let you waste your time at any of them. In this little guide you'll find our opinion on the very best places for the design-minded, food-focused, nature-loving explorers of the city – whether you're here for a weekend or forever.

Partial to art stencilled on a street corner? Book onto a Banksy walking tour or head down to North Street to see the murals made at Upfest (no.44). Prefer to see it hung on a Grade II-listed wall? The Royal West of England Academy (no.40) awaits. Want to paddle in restored Victorian swimming baths? Snap up a spot at the Bristol Lido (no.39). Or in an artificial surf lake? Venture out to The Wave (no.38). Eco-friendly options to eat aren't restricted to restaurants that win Michelin Green Stars (though Wilsons does have one, no.17): you'll find seasonal menus in brunch spots (The Bristol Loaf, no.6), ethically sourced Sunday roasts on boats (The Grain Barge, no.52) and biodynamic wine lists in shipping containers (Wapping Wharf, no.22). And Bristol's history isn't only brought to life by famous landmarks (like the Clifton Suspension Bridge, no.46), but by local people – head to the M Shed museum (no.42) to hear their stories.

Of course, it would be impossible to cram all of Bristol's ebullient essence into a book you can fit in your pocket. Instead, we've picked out 60 of the most vibrant spots where you can eat, drink, dance, look, learn, shop, swim, surf, cycle and even set sail right in the city, so you can enjoy some of Bristol's independent spirit without ever crossing paths with a stag do.

Florence Filose,
Bristol, 2023

A PERFECT WEEKEND

Friday night

Check into the Artist Residence Bristol (no.59) to start your city break in style (and a central location), then head straight out to Bokman (no.7) for soju-infused cocktails, Korean drinking snacks and bowls of bibimbap before seeing who's playing live at The Canteen (no.54).

Saturday morning

Pick up pastries for the road from Farro (no.9) – it would be rude not to when you're right next door – then head up to Gloucester Road for coffee (or a second breakfast) at Fed (no.11). Wander back down past some of Bristol's best indie shops, popping in to browse greenery in Wild Leaf (no.33) or garments in The Ottowin Shop (no.26) and Fox + Feather (no.25).

Saturday lunch

Treat yourself to the tasting menu at Wilsons (no.17) or keep it simple with a bowl of fresh pasta from Little Hollows Pasta Co. (no.10) next door, before walking it off with a stroll through Clifton to admire Bristol's most famous bridge (no.46).

Saturday afternoon

Stop by Heron Books (no.32) for some reading material on your way to Bristol Lido (no.39), where you can sit outside with a cold beer while swimmers glide past, or head to Royal West of England Academy (no.40) to soak up some art instead.

Saturday night

Share some small plates at Marmo (no.1) before catching a show at whichever one of Bristol's best cultural hotspots most takes your fancy: a film screening at the Watershed (no.45), a play at Bristol Old Vic (no.47) or a gig at Bristol Beacon (no.57).

Sunday brunch

Time for a lie in, before venturing south for sourdough crumpets from The Bristol Loaf (no.6) and an amble down North Street, calling in at Upfest Gallery (no.44) and Mon Pote (no.27) before perusing the stalls at the Tobacco Factory's (no.50) Sunday market.

Sunday afternoon

Head over to the docks for a scenic saunter, ending up at Underfall Yard (no.48) to hear about the harbour's history, or the M Shed (no.42) to explore even more of the city's past and present. Circle round for a late Sunday lunch at the Grain Barge (no.52) or take your pick of cuisines from the restaurants housed in Wapping Wharf's shipping containers (no.22).

Sunday night

Toast the end of your weekend with a brewed-on-site beer at Left Handed Giant (no.55) or, if you're still going strong, catch an experimental performance at The Wardrobe Theatre in The Old Market Assembly (no.56).

AREAS TO EXPLORE

Centre & Old City
Here you'll find Bristol's oldest cobbled alleys alongside its newest shiny shopping centre, Cabot Circus, as well as Park Street's notoriously steep incline.

Hotwells & Harbourside
Hotwells' oft-photographed colourful houses sit above the floating harbour, a fascinating piece of Bristol's engineering history that still bustles with boats and waterbuses.

Clifton, Cotham & Redland
Clifton Village's picturesque Georgian and Victorian terraces offer dramatic views over the city backed by a cliffside stretch of protected parkland. Neighbouring Cotham and Redland are both known for their leafy streets and thriving food scenes.

Gloucester Road,
Stokes Croft & St Pauls
Gloucester Road, the UK's longest stretch of independent shops, leads down to countercultural hub Stokes Croft and next-door St Pauls, which holds its famous African Caribbean carnival each summer.

Old Market & Easton
The historic architecture of Old Market spans over 60 listed buildings, now home to antique shops and buzzing bars, while Easton has both an array of indie eateries and a vibrant community high street, St Marks Road.

Redcliffe, Totterdown & Arnos Vale
Bristol's Brunel-designed main train station, Temple Meads, sits in rapidly regenerating Redcliffe. To the south, Totterdown's streets of multi-hued houses border Arnos Vale's 45-acre Victorian cemetery and Paintworks creative quarter.

Bedminster & Southville
South of the river, creative shops and cafes line each side of North Street which snakes through Southville and Bedminster towards the grassy, undulating expanse of Victoria Park.

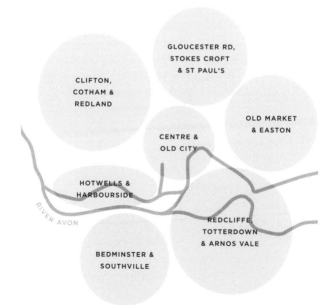

GLOUCESTER RD, STOKES CROFT & ST PAUL'S

CLIFTON, COTHAM & REDLAND

OLD MARKET & EASTON

CENTRE & OLD CITY

HOTWELLS & HARBOURSIDE

RIVER AVON

REDCLIFFE, TOTTERDOWN & ARNOS VALE

BEDMINSTER & SOUTHVILLE

1

MARMO

Stylish Italian-accented restaurant and wine bar

Tucked between the streets of the Old City, Marmo is exactly the kind of place you want to spend a Friday night – buzzy location, convivial clientele and a menu made for sharing with a bottle of something delicious. The food list is concise; the wine menu is longer. Ask the friendly staff what to try from a selection including naturally fermented Proseccos, organic rosés, single-vineyard reds and much, much more. Accompany what you're drinking with crisp, melt-in-the-mouth gnocco fritto, steak tartare on toast or perfectly al dente pasta and you're sure to start your weekend right.

31 Baldwin Street, BS1 1RG
marmo.restaurant

2

THE GARDEN OF EASTON

Neighbourhood restaurant for global cuisine

Garden by name, garden by nature: this spot in Easton is full to the rafters with hanging plants and curling vines. You might even spot a (fake) pigeon perched high above the diners. Brunch options range from Turkish eggs to Japanese pancakes, while at night they serve small plates and switch on fairy lights among the leaves. Grab a spot to sample artichoke hearts on whipped miso tofu or sticky, crispy aubergine with kecap manis (a sweet Indonesian soy sauce) washed down with a smoked mezcal margarita. The menu skips around the globe, but the produce is all sourced locally.

89 St Marks Road, BS5 6HY
thegardenofeaston.co.uk

3

NUTMEG

A celebration of regional Indian cooking

Set between Georgian terraces, this vibrant Indian restaurant is a welcome stop-off after an afternoon spent exploring the picturesque hilltop walkways of Clifton Village. Inside, multicoloured murals span the walls, embroidered umbrellas twirl above your head and the mouth-watering smell of spices fills the air. The menu takes inspiration from all over India, offering Punjabi chana masala alongside Bihari tarka daal and Goan vindaloo, accompanied by plump naan and fragrant saffron rice. Finish with a traditional sweet gulab jamun (syrup-steeped, deep-fried dough balls), or crack into the aromatic fusion of a chai-spiced crème brûlée.

10 The Mall, BS8 4DR
Other location: City Centre
nutmegbristol.com

4

BIANCHIS

Lively trattoria for delicious Italian fare

Montpelier was bereft when neighbourhood favourite Bell's Diner closed its doors in 2019 after more than 40 years, but thankfully it wasn't long before the family-run Bianchis Group, some of Bristol's most respected restaurateurs, picked up the baton. This homely haunt is once again a favourite spot for candlelit dates and family occasions, thanks to its rustic interiors and refined Italian plates. The menu is best served shared: a few antipasti for the table, followed by steaming bowls of cacio e pepe or truffle agnolotti for primi, expertly cooked cuts of meat or fish for secondi and a slither of rich chocolate tart to end, all accompanied by a bottle of fine Italian red. Saluti!

1–3 York Road, BS6 5QB
bianchisrestaurant.co.uk

5

PACO TAPAS

Modern tapas from heritage Spanish flavours

Family-run Paco takes traditional tapas and gives it a decidedly high-end twist. Chef Peter Sanchez-Iglesias uses the flavours of his heritage to create plates of exquisitely crispy patatas bravas, garlic-drenched *gambas* and fluffy tortilla Española, with specials of the day scrawled on paper menus and a list of handpicked sherries. The setting is a network of black-bricked walls and archways, which – with the smell of wood smoke in the air – feels straight out of Andalusia, but picturesque views of boats and coloured houses from the rather nice outside area will remind you that you're still in Bristol.

3a Lower Guinea Street, BS1 6FU
pacotapas.co.uk

Tostada de Tomate 6.5
... fondo en ... 5
... 5
... apples 5

PACO
6 My 2022

Para picar

Smoked Almonds
Pimientos Marin...
Gorda Olives
Manzanilla ...
Bread & Ol...
Boqueror...
Tortilla F...
Manche...

Cold

Chorizo
Valdella
salchin...
Lomo de...

Croquet...

Jamon...

Stew

Huevos a la Flam...

Vegetable

Patatas Bravas
leeks and Rome...
Ensalada de To...
Devilled ch...

Quesos

...ono de Zuh...
Tata De...

Postres

Crema Catalana
Chocolate mous...
pedro xi...
sour ch...

6

THE BRISTOL LOAF

Bedminster favourite for brunch, bread and bakes

Don't be fooled by its moniker – The Bristol Loaf does a whole lot more than bread. On weekends, there's often a queue out the door as Bedminster's brunchers wait to sample simple comforts like freshly baked sourdough crumpets with cultured butter, Loaf's signature 'croilinders' (croissant cups with seasonal fillings) or adventurous specials like whipped ewe's curd and candied walnuts on toast. Of course, you *can* also pick up an organic loaf here – as well as a bottle of something interesting from the in-house natural wine shop, The Bristol Vine.

96 Bedminster Parade, BS3 4HL
Other locations: Redfield, Bristol Beacon (no.57)
thebristolloaf.co.uk

7

BOKMAN

Sensational Korean food in spare surroundings

There's a supper-club atmosphere to this snug Korean joint just off Stokes Croft: the food choices are chalked on a blackboard, the decor is minimal and the staff chat you through the menu like old friends. The star of the show is the succulent, crispy-skinned *tongdak*: a whole rotisserie chicken stuffed with sticky rice that makes a mouth-watering centre piece for two, paired with pickles and dipping sauces. But don't miss out on the other authentic flavours husband-and-wife team Duncan Robertson and Kyu Jeong Jeon are showcasing here, from a bibimbap bowl so piping hot that you can see the rice caramelising before your eyes, to the indisputably best kimchi in Bristol.

3 Nine Tree Hill, BS1 3SB
instagram.com/bokmanbristol

8

HART'S BAKERY

Artisan bakers below a bustling station

Planning to arrive or depart Bristol by train? Do all you can to factor a visit to Hart's into your itinerary. Rather incongruously located in a carpark beneath the station, this brilliant bakery hand-makes some of the freshest bread, cakes and pastries you can buy in Bristol using fastidiously sourced flour and exciting seasonal flavours, alongside a different wholesome lunch special each weekday. From rhubarb friands in spring to delightfully autumnal toffee apple doughnuts, all Hart's delectable goods are baked within their Victorian railway arch and sold, temptingly golden, straight from the oven.

Arch 35, Lower Approach Road, BS1 6QS
hartsbakery.co.uk

9

FARRO

Rightly renowned bakery

You'll have to forego your weekend lie-in to get the goods at Farro: this nationally acclaimed bakery is so popular that a queue snakes out the door each morning, and by midday most of the stock has been bagged. But when that stock is made up of twice-baked honey and almond pastries, glossy chocolate babkas, crisp caramelly kouign-amann and the flakiest, most velvety pastéis de nata this side of Portugal, it's not hard to see what's got everyone up so early. Farro's location on the side of an A-road isn't quite as beautiful as its bakes and the seating inside is minimal, so it's best to grab a bag to take away and head back for breakfast in bed.

1 Brunswick Square (facing onto Bond Street), BS2 8PE
instagram.com/farrobakery

10

LITTLE HOLLOWS PASTA CO.

Fantastic fresh pasta

Pasta-partisans, you'll know you're in good hands as soon as you arrive at Little Hollows – where you can watch the chefs in the front window feeding huge sheets of dough through a machine, or piping neat lines of fresh fillings (including roasted celeriac and pickled walnut or pulled skate wing and chopped scallop). The linguine (or tagliatelle or bucatini or rigatoni) are drenched in satisfying sauces from mint and basil pesto to lamb shank ragù, mopped up with hunks of sourdough from Hart's (no.8). The pasta may be the main event, but don't get so caught up in the carb consumption that you forget to leave room for head chef Flo's signature hazelnut tiramisu – washed down with a shot of homemade limoncello.

26 Chandos Road, BS6 6PF
littlehollowspasta.co.uk

11

FED

Cafes with cornucopian countertops

The interiors of this much-loved Bristolian mini chain are strikingly minimalist. The counters, on the other hand, are nothing but maximalist. An unbelievably abundant display of breads and salads, tarts and pastries, cookies and cakes, buns, brownies and beyond greets you at every outpost. Visit the biggest branch on Gloucester Road for the full menu of hot brunch and lunch dishes and the option of eating in the courtyard out back, pop by the cosiest cafe just off Cotham Hill for a wholesome bowl of overnight oats or stop for coffee and cake at the light-flooded space in Fishponds. It will take more than a few visits to try every delicious thing on offer.

313 Gloucester Road, BS7 8PE
Other locations: Fishponds, Cotham
fedcafe.co.uk

12

FULL COURT PRESS

A speciality coffee shop for everyone

Is good coffee a science or an art? At Full Court Press, it's both. Behind the stripped-back wooden counter, baristas attend to funnels and flasks that wouldn't look out of place in a lab, while the walls are adorned with framed packets from an array of roasters in place of pictures. You might think that all sounds offputtingly hipster, but fear not – no one here will sneer if you prefer a milky latte to a fashionable filter. Instead, the impressively knowledgeable staff will talk you through the range of roasts scrawled on the board that day, so you can choose exactly how you want to enjoy them.

59 Broad Street, BS1 2EJ
fcp.coffee

13

COR

Mouthwatering Mediterranean small plates

COR resides behind one of North Street's most vivid exteriors, adorned with abstract botanical shapes that Bristol artist Sophie Rae created during Upfest (no.44). The food is every bit as vibrant as the walls outside. The small (plus a few big) plates menu takes its influence from all around the Mediterranean, presenting simple produce with complex depth and artful innovation – like their savoury canelé, a playful twist on the usually caramelised French pastry. The food may be seriously good, but the atmosphere is casually welcoming: expect cook book-lined walls and window seating, so you can pull up a stool and watch Bedminster go by.

81 North Street, BS3 1ES
correstaurant.com

14

BURRA

Brunch from down under

If Burra's name and kookaburra logo don't tip you off to its Antipodean theme, its shelves by the door lined with Tim Tams and Vegemite certainly will. As is fitting for an Aussie brunch spot, the interiors are chilled-out and light-filled. Options for things to have on toast are plentiful – smashed avo, poached eggs, salmon scramble – alongside colourful rice bowls and expertly steamed flat whites. But it's not just the sunshine-infused menu that's piqued interest in Burra: owners Luke Morahan and Jake Heenan were better known for playing for the Bristol Bears rugby team before they gave the brunch business a *try* (sorry).

7 Lower Redland Road, BS6 6TB
Other location: Southville
burrabristol.co.uk

15

LITTLEFRENCH

Unashamedly indulgent French fare

Among Bristol's abundance of small-plate, plant-focused restaurants, littlefrench feels defiantly, deliciously different. Drizzled in butter, dripping with melted cheese and accompanied by towering piles of salty frites and punchy aioli, the plates here forego lightness in favour of deep, decadent flavour – all served in a cosy bistro setting lit by hanging lanterns. From starters of twice-baked soufflé Suissesse or milk-fed lamb sweetbreads to sharing plates of whole roast guinea fowl or wood-grilled côte de bœuf, everything is rich, juicy and generously portioned. Stick a napkin in your collar and get stuck in.

2 North View, Westbury Park, BS6 7QB
littlefrench.co.uk

16

FLOUR & ASH

Sourdough pizzas wood-fired before your eyes

May the pineapple-on-pizza debate finally be laid to rest, for this powderpuff-pink pizzeria in Clifton could convince even the most vehement sceptic. The Parma & Pineapple, with crispy ham and caramelised pineapple, is just one highlight of a toppings menu that also includes the Honey Roast Pumpkin Pie with gorgonzola, and Slow-cooked Lamb Shoulder sprinkled with feta. This focus on artisan flavours means Flour & Ash is slightly pricier than your average pizza palace, but the offer of free kids' meals between 12–5pm on weekdays makes it a great spot for families to save some dough.

50 Whiteladies Road, BS8 2NH
flourandashbristol.com

17

WILSONS

Seasonal restaurant with its own smallholding

The walls at Wilsons are bare other than two chalkboards: one showing that day's set menu opposite another with the wine list. It makes sense, because both menus are in themselves works of art. Created in dialogue with the seasons, the six courses served daily are built around what's growing in Wilsons' market garden (which is just 20 minutes away) as well as fastidiously sourced meat and seafood, paired with low-intervention wines from small-scale makers. Visit on a weekday (Wednesday to Friday) to enjoy the deliciously good value of a shortened lunch menu.

24 Chandos Road, BS6 6PF
wilsonsbristol.co.uk

18

SWOON GELATO

Family-owned gelateria for authentic Italian scoops

Sicilian pistachios, hazelnuts from Piedmont, Amarena cherries… On Swoon's glass counter sits a taste tour of Italy, folded into sumptuously creamy gelato or blended through smooth sorbetti. The slow-churned, authentically made ices pay homage to the heritage of the shop's founders, the Forte family, who learned their trade from their grandparents, Nonno Alfonso and Nonna Adelina. Still, the Fortes aren't afraid to step outside of tradition in the name of indulgence: expect monthly guest flavours and ice cream creations like the chocolate-drizzled, wafer-topped 'Tiramiswoondae'.

31 College Green, BS1 5TB
Other location: Wapping Wharf (no.22)
swoononaspoon.co.uk

19
AHH TOOTS

Sweet treats on a sweet street

Once a favourite stall at St Nicks Market (no.30), these days this creative cakery has a permanent home on one of Bristol's loveliest streets. Found in a quirky Tudor-fronted building at the bottom of the Christmas Steps (a stepped shopping street whose history dates back to medieval times), Ahh Toots is now a resident of the city's celebrated arts quarter. The tiny wood-panelled sitting room is about the cutest place imaginable to eat cake, though on Saturdays you'll need to book in for afternoon tea – not a hard ask when that means indulging in delicacies like spiced carrot choux buns, earl grey macarons and sour cherry scones.

17 Christmas Street, BS1 5BT
ahhtoots.com

20

ADELINA YARD

Fuss-free and friendly fine dining

Granted, a three-hour, ten-course tasting menu isn't everyone's idea of a good time. But if you are the sort to get swept away by a procession of increasingly exquisite morsels, there are few better places than Adelina Yard. Opened in 2015 by chefs Olivia Barry and Jamie Randall, both of whom worked in Michelin-starred London restaurants, Adelina Yard makes fine dining the theatrical experience it should be. In its bright, wood-accented dining room, the flavours are as intricate as the service is straightforward and unstuffy. If you're not the tasting menu type, you can always go for lunch instead, when the menu is kept to a mere four courses.

Queen's Quay, BS1 4SL
adelinayard.com

21

UNDER THE STARS

Hidden gem on the hectic harbourside

Under the Stars isn't misnamed: this boat-bar is the perfect place to sit beneath a twinkling sky and put the world to rights while working your way through their cocktail menu. But don't get so carried away by the top deck that you forget to venture down below to the rather lovely hidden restaurant. Although the boat is moored in one of Harbourside's busiest thoroughfares, the timber-panelled dining room feels cosy and intimate, lit by candles stuffed into gin bottles and festoons of fairy lights. The menu is mainly Mediterranean tapas: plates of spiced tiger prawns, padron peppers and patatas bravas add to the warm atmosphere.

Narrow Quay, BS1 4QA
underthestarsbar.co.uk

22

WAPPING WHARF

An indie shipping-container community

Beware, those who are easily overwhelmed by choice: Wapping Wharf crams a frankly daunting number of Bristol's finest shops and restaurants into a single harbourside spot. The only antidote to this inundation is spending an entire afternoon here. Browse the shelves of Bookhaus, sample West Country delights at The Bristol Cheesemonger (try the cider-washed Yarlington) or peruse vintage finds at Something Elsie. But then you still need to decide where to go for dinner – will it be Root's veg-celebrating small plates, sushi from Seven Lucky Gods or a fish-and-chip takeaway from Salt & Malt? You'll just have to hope Bristol's beloved Free Silent Disco turns up outside so you can dance off the indecision.

Wapping Road, BS1 4RW
wappingwharf.co.uk

23

KOOCHA MEZZE BAR

Plant-based Persian plates

Creamy whipped feta, fresh tzatziki, doner-stuffed bao buns and saffron cheesecake – glance at the menu of this mural-covered mezze restaurant and you won't clock that everything on it is plant-based. In fact, Koocha was Bristol's first ever totally vegan restaurant and has been a stalwart for inventive, affordable, ethical eating since 2018. The laidback, lively atmosphere makes it a great place to share some plates (and a couple of spiced cocktails) with friends before heading to the nearby Canteen (no.54) for dancing till late. Head back the next morning for a fully loaded 'Koocha Breakfast' – a Middle Eastern-inspired fry-up that will cure any sore head.

203B Cheltenham Road, BS6 5QX
koochamezzebar.com

24

GOOD STORE STUDIO

Indie lifestyle shop that's thrice as nice

Good Store Studio is the brainchild of three friends: Josie, Emma and Beth. The trio each use their own style to stock the shop with the best independent brands and studio makers, from hand-painted ceramics to small-batch beauty products, as well as glorious garments from Josie and Emma's own businesses. At the in-store studio, Josie sews made-to-measure outfits and fills a colourful corner of the shop with linen co-ords and contrasting corduroys, while Emma turns discarded duvet covers into unique unisex outfits featuring whimsical patterns and nostalgic prints.

31 Old Market Street, BS2 0HB
goodstorestudio.co.uk

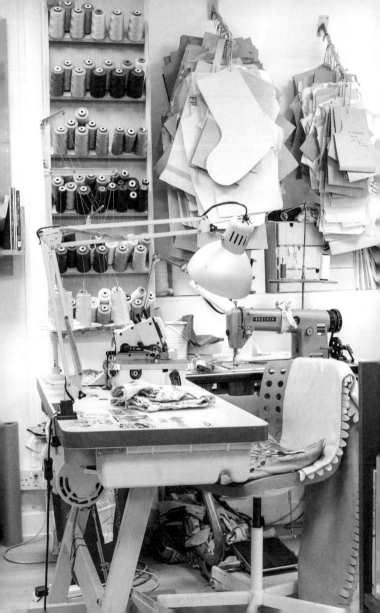

25

FOX + FEATHER

Clothes shop for wonderful womenswear

Struggling with your sartorial style? A visit to Fox + Feather is in order. This little boutique has stocked its rails with a riot of colour, texture and sparkle from sought-after cosmopolitan brands, while keeping the prices happily high street. Pick up a party dress from Danish designer Nümph, an embroidered blouse from women-founded brand seventy + mochi or add some effortless elegance to your wardrobe with a slouchy knit from FRNCH. Labels mean little to you? No matter, the store's friendly staff are on hand to help you put together an outfit that will make you feel great.

41 Gloucester Road, BS7 8AD
foxandfeather.co.uk

26

THE OTTOWIN SHOP

Exquisite shoes made on-site

Even in a city where the words 'locally made' are practically ubiquitous, The Ottowin Shop steps things up – by allowing you to step *out* in shoes that are made not just in the city, but actually inside the shop. Ottowin's gorgeous footwear is handcrafted by the founders in their in-store studio, often using industry offcuts and hand-painted leathers, in batches of less than 200 per year. Browse clothes and jewellery from other brands who love traditional methods as much as Ottowin, then sign up for a shoe-making course to join in the slow production revolution from the ground up.

56 Gloucester Road, BS7 8BH
theottowin.shop

27

MON POTE

Infinitely browsable Scandinavian homewares

Awash with earthen tones and pleasing pastels, the careful curation of this independent lifestyle shop on vibrant North Street makes it a place to find inspiration, as well as some subtly hued new glassware. The in-store selection changes with the seasons, but the continuity comes from a focus on setting the best in Scandi styling alongside West Country makers. 'Mon Pote' translates as 'my friend' – but, giftable as its homewares may be, you might find yourself unwilling to part with any new purchase.

217a North Street, BS3 1JJ
monpote.co.uk

28

STOKES CROFT CHINA

Homeware that resists convention

Prefer your political statements printed on bone china? This unique shop is the place for you. Run by the People's Republic of Stokes Croft, a community organisation dedicated to keeping the Stokes Croft spirit of creative dissent alive and kicking, here you'll find a potted history of Bristolian activism fired onto ceramics of all sorts. Their defiant designs span witty critiques of the government to impassioned advocacy for nature and the NHS (with some pissed-off cats thrown in for good measure), combining salvaged prints with modern motifs by local artists. And if statement tableware isn't your thing, a mug from their beautiful 'Bristol Blue Rose' range still makes the perfect souvenir.

35 Jamaica Street, BS2 8JP
prscshop.co.uk

29

BAM STORE + SPACE

Colourful wares and workshops

In 2019, Easton local Fran Harkness was looking for a way to support and showcase her neighbourhood's creative community, so she opened BAM: a non-profit shop and event space dedicated to doing just that. Now, locals and out-of-towners alike can tap into BAM's buzz by joining one its eclectic workshops, which range from darning lessons to collage club social nights. No time to stop and stitch? You can still take the Easton energy home with you in the form of a leopard-print bumbag or some fresh new stationery – or choose from the gallery wall of neon-hued prints and risographs, many of which are specially commissioned from Bristol artists.

104–108 Belle Vue Road, BS5 6BX
bambristol.co.uk

30

ST NICHOLAS MARKET

Atmospheric indoor market

There's a sense of history to the hubbub in St Nicks – people have been trading here ever since 1743. Back then it was only corn that was exchanged, but nowadays you can get your hands on just about anything courtesy of the more than 60 colourful stalls. Ceramics and spices jostle for space with fossils and gemstones, handmade leather goods sit beside hand-carved wooden instruments and the Glass Arcade out back is home to street food vendors selling an assortment of global cuisines. It's worth a visit for the atmosphere alone (as well as the stuffed-to-bursting falafel pittas), especially on Fridays and Saturdays when even more indie traders spill out onto Corn Street.

The Corn Exchange, Corn Street, BS1 1JQ
bristol.gov.uk/st-nicholas-markets

31

TEMPLE CYCLES

Beautiful Bristol-built bikes

If you're going to huff, puff and pedal your way up Park Street, you might as well do it in style – and there's truly no more stylish way than on a Temple. But this Bristol-founded bikemaker isn't only about looks: Temple's lightweight steel frames, sustainable ethos and classic, comfortable designs make riding them truly enjoyable, whether you're commuting into the city or heading out to explore the Somerset trails. Book in for a test ride at their workshop on the outskirts of Bristol where each of their bikes is hand-assembled, and try one for yourself.

Unit 22 Brookgate Trading Estate, BS3 2UN
templecycles.co.uk

32

HERON BOOKS

Indie bookshop in a reclaimed Victorian arcade

Clifton's only independent bookshop has been welcoming readers to browse its thoughtfully chosen selection since 2022, but its historic environs have been serving shoppers for – well, actually, not as long as you might expect. Architect Joseph King's arcade was first completed in 1878, but it fell almost instantly into disuse – leading to its nickname 'King's Folly'. For decades, it was a storage depot until its eventual restoration and reopening in 1998. A visit to Heron now offers up multiple unearthed gems: both the resurrected Bristol Venetian arcade, and the offbeat reading recommendations happily divulged by friendly booksellers.

Unit 5, The Clifton Arcade, BS8 4AA
heronbooks.co.uk

33

WILD LEAF

Peaceful plant store

Wild Leaf believe houseplants can help our mental health. It's hard to disagree with them: as soon as you step off busy Gloucester Road into their dark-walled, greenery-filled sanctum, you feel instantly more at ease. Bring some of this serenity home with you by perusing their selection of gleaming monsteras, interesting succulents, trailing vines, botanical books and stylish pots. Staff are super knowledgeable about the plants they sell, and will talk you through all your leafy new friend's needs so you can keep it looking as lush and glossy as it did on the shelf.

43 Gloucester Road, BS7 8AD
wildleafbristol.co.uk

34

BRISTOL AND BATH RAILWAY PATH

Easy cycling through bucolic scenery

Once the tracks of the Midland Railway, this tree-shaded path provides a flat walking and cycling route from Bristol to Bath. The 13-mile ride takes you through the picturesque Avon Valley, under bridges, past cute cafes and through a disused railway tunnel. For pit-stops, begin with coffee and croissants from Bakehouse at the path's start, stop for toasties at Bath Soft Cheese around the ten-mile mark (look out for a farm track on the left, just after the bridge at Saltford) and finish with a pint from the Electric Bear brewery on the outskirts of Bath – then book the bikes onto a train back to Bristol to avoid a wobbly cycle home.

Starts at: St Philips Road, BS2 0NT
bristolbathrailwaypath.org.uk

35
CABOT TOWER & BRANDON HILL

Hilltop oasis in the centre of the city

Bristol is a city of hills: there's no avoiding them. So, if you're *going* to schlep up a taxing incline, you might as well make it all the way to Brandon Hill. Bristol's oldest park, this tree-shaded plot of weaving pathways and open vistas is an unbeatable spot for a picnic. From its apex rises the ornate red-sandstone Cabot Tower, built in 1897 to commemorate 400 years since *The Matthew* (no.36) set sail. And once you're there, why *not* climb 108 steps of the tower's (quite claustrophobic) spiral staircase? You'll be rewarded with panoramic views of the city and (yet more) rolling hills beyond.

Park Street, BS1 5RR
Free access

36

THE MATTHEW
OF BRISTOL

Real deal sailing trips on a replica ship

Whether you've a brood of young mariners or are partial to a sea shanty yourself, family days out don't get much heartier than this. Modelled on the wooden vessel that explorer John Cabot chartered to cross the Atlantic in 1497, *The Matthew* has been painstakingly constructed to be as close to a 15th-century ship as possible – albeit with the addition of a fully licensed bar. Climb aboard for a free tour while it's moored, set off on a 'fish and chips trip' around the harbour, or voyage out to the River Avon, gazing up at the celebrated Clifton Suspension Bridge (no.46) as you sail beneath it.

Princes Wharf, BS1 4RN
matthew.co.uk

37

ASHTON COURT ESTATE

Bucolic hills beneath balloon-filled skies

Only a ten-minute bus ride from the city centre, these 850 acres of wooded parkland offer an eclectic range of pastoral pursuits – including a tree-top obstacle course, a Grade I-listed mansion that does a great flat white, two deer parks, a miniature railway and even a FootGolf course for those who just can't decide if they'd rather play football or golf (we've all been there). There's also plenty of space to simply roam in peace and admire the spectacular views over the city – augmented each August by the Bristol International Balloon Fiesta, when up to a hundred hot air balloons make a mass ascent over the verdant Estate.

Long Ashton, BS41 9JN
Free access, some paid activities

38

THE WAVE

Pioneering land-locked surf spot

Something strange is going on in the suburbs of Bristol. Six-foot waves are breaking in the middle of a farm, far from the ocean. *How* is anyone's guess – the technology is top secret – but *why* is obvious: it's miraculously, exhilaratingly fun. The first of its kind in the UK, The Wave is on a mission to improve city-dwellers' access to 'blue space' and its mental health benefits while using 100 per cent renewable energy. The lake's guaranteed surf offers something for everyone, with different wave heights for varying abilities, plus bodyboarding and swimming sessions for those who just want to play in the breakers.

Washingpool Farm, BS35 5RE
thewave.com

39

BRISTOL LIDO

A sunny holiday without leaving the West Country

Why risk flight delays when a Spanish oasis awaits on a residential road in Clifton? In the pool-side bar at Bristol Lido, you can knock back salty Cantabrian anchovies and sip a chilled Alhambra Reserva while clear blue waters lap at your feet. Dipping in you may find the 'ocean' slightly chillier than the Costa del Sol, but at least the heated pool is still bracing enough to make a post-swim plunge in the outdoor hot tub mandatory. The best way to visit is to book a swim-and-dine package ahead of time as swimming spaces for non-members fill up quickly, and the waiting list for membership is (perhaps understandably) over a thousand people long.

Oakfield Place, BS8 2BJ
lidobristol.com

40

ROYAL WEST OF ENGLAND ACADEMY

Landmark gallery that's inspiring inside and out

Bristol's original art gallery, the RWA is as lovely to look at as the works within it. The listed building was purpose-built in 1857, largely thanks to the patronage of pioneering English painter Ellen Sharples. What's on show changes throughout the year, with annual highlights including the Open Exhibition, when a multitude of mediums jostle for space across the galleries, and the Secret Postcard Auction, where bidding on anonymous miniature masterpieces starts from just £40. Its recent renovation added a family activity room (where the dressing-up wall features a unicorn cape and a Yayoi Kusama costume) and a cafe piled high with savoury bakes from local lunch maestros, Spicer+Cole.

Queens Road, BS8 1PX
rwa.org.uk

41

SPIKE ISLAND

Contemporary art in a much-loved locale

This creative community hub is named after the historic strip of industrial dockland it sits upon between the River Avon and Bristol Floating Harbour. Alongside fostering a coterie of local artists in its studios, the gallery brings contemporary art from around the globe to an exhibition space that feels truly welcoming – thoughtful children's activity sheets encourage younger visitors to creatively engage with each artist's medium and message. It's free to visit (with donations encouraged) and the attached cafe, Emmeline, is a cut above the usual gallery pitstops with colourful salads, smoothies and self-proclaimed 'mega cheese toasties'.

133 Cumberland Road, BS1 6UX
spikeisland.org.uk

42

M SHED

Discover Bristol's past, present and future

At this dockside museum housed in a 1950s transit shed and flanked by cargo cranes, Bristol's story is told not just through its big names – Brunel, Banksy, Wallace and Gromit – but by its residents. Walk all over the huge map of the city (learning about its neighbourhoods firsthand from locals) or explore the miscellany of interesting objects upstairs, from preserved protest placards to Fry's chocolate packaging (the first mass-produced bar was made in the city). There is also a frank exhibition on Bristol's historic involvement in the transatlantic slave trade. With plenty of places to have your say or interact with exhibits, the M Shed explores the city's past to enrich its future.

Princes Wharf, Wapping Road, BS1 4RN
bristolmuseums.org.uk/m-shed

43

WAKE THE TIGER

Another dimension of immersive art

Somewhere between an art trail and a hallucino-genic experience, Wake the Tiger is a labyrinthine series of spaces each more minutely detailed than the last. Stroll from an enchanted forest where luminous flowers flutter above your head to a glittering rock cavern cut through with neon portals, find secret doorways hidden behind bookcases and manip-ulate steampunk machines to create otherworldly sounds. The endless exploration makes it perfect for kids and adults alike – with plenty of photo opportunities. Attempt to piece together the story of the alternate world of Meridia where a mysterious people are battling to save their ecosystem – or simply wander in wonder from room to room.

127 Albert Road, BS2 0YA
wakethetiger.com

44

UPFEST

Open-air art and urban gallery

Bristol may be best known for Banksy, but the city's street art culture extends far beyond its most mysterious artist. Take a wander down North Street and you'll pass all manner of amazing murals sprayed above the shopfronts. The artworks are made as part of Upfest, Europe's largest street art festival: on their website you'll find a map with info on each piece. Usually a highlight in Bristol's cultural calendar, rising costs are sadly threatening the future of Upfest's annual festival weekend. Support them by visiting their permanent gallery in Bedminster, where you can also peruse a vast range of urban art-making materials.

Gallery: 198 North Street, BS3 1JF
upfest.co.uk

45

WATERSHED

A meeting place for movie lovers

Anyone who thinks cinema is dead hasn't been to the Watershed on a weekday. This harbourside hangout is a haven for film culture that champions inclusive arts education – while also serving up colossal plates of loaded nachos in its buzzing bar. Screenings span experimental indie pictures, hot new releases and crowd-pleasing oldies, plus, tickets are (unusually for cinemas nowadays) reasonably priced. They even run baby-friendly screenings. It's not just the weekly programme that feels thoughtfully curated: a rotating range of craft beers and ciders on tap mean you can discover the best in world cinema while sipping on a local brew.

1 Canons Road, BS1 5TX
watershed.co.uk

46

CLIFTON SUSPENSION BRIDGE

Brunel's Bristol icon

Only a few cities in the world can boast of a bridge so famous, it's worth seeing even if you don't end up crossing it. San Francisco has the Golden Gate, Florence has the Ponte Vecchio – and Bristol has the Clifton Suspension Bridge. Designed by Isambard Kingdom Brunel and first opened in 1864, it spans the imposing crags of the Avon Gorge connecting Clifton to the beauty of Leigh Woods, and has become a symbol of Bristol's creative spirit. It's free to cross for cyclists and pedestrians and, with excellent coffee from Chapter & Holmes available on both sides, it's well worth the wander – as long as you don't have vertigo.

Visitor Centre: Bridge Road, BS8 3PA
cliftonbridge.org.uk

47

BRISTOL OLD VIC

Historic theatre putting on modern shows

The Bristol Old Vic proudly declares itself to be the oldest continuously working theatre in the English-speaking world – not that you'd know it, from the multi-million-pound redevelopment its front of house underwent in 2016. In the dramatically designed new foyer, soaring timber structures offset the weathered original façade of the Georgian auditorium, and the improved space (as well as the menu of gravy-drenched deliciousness from local pastry-connoisseurs, Pieminister) has turned the Old Vic into a community hub as well as an award-winning theatre. Its programme ranges from classic shows with a playful twist to innovative new writing, as well as an ever-changing selection of riotous children's theatre – allowing every age group to discover, or rediscover, their love of the stage.

King Street, BS1 4ED
bristololdvic.org.uk

48

UNDERFALL YARD

200-year-old boatyard with a great cafe

Whether you're up for deepening your knowledge of hydraulic power or simply want to sit with a coffee and bacon bap in hand and admire one of the harbour's prettiest viewpoints, Underfall Yard is a must-visit on any stroll around the docks. In the visitor centre (once the harbour's powerhouse), interactive exhibits and enthusiastic volunteers manage to make silt-drainage fascinating, while explaining the Yard's important place in Bristol's history. It's still a working boatyard, though a fire in 2023 destroyed many of its workshops. The Underfall Yard Trust is working hard to restore this special site to its once-bustling glory – even more reason to lend them your patronage.

Cumberland Road, BS1 6XG
underfallyard.co.uk

49

MARTIN PARR FOUNDATION

Iconic photographer's photobook archive

Beloved Bristol-based photographer Martin Parr has long been a champion of the photobook, having published around 40 of his own. It's no surprise therefore that the Martin Parr Foundation (the charity, gallery and archive Parr founded in 2014) is a veritable treasure trove of them. Alongside Parr's own tomes of intimate, irony-infused documentary photographs, you'll find publications from indie presses, emerging artists and established photographers, all on the subject of Britain and Ireland. The library, which holds over 5,000 photobooks, is primarily available to members (you can sign up online), but the gallery is free for all – and its gift shop is a collection in itself.

316 Paintworks, BS4 3AR
martinparrfoundation.org

50

TOBACCO FACTORY

A theatre-slash-farm shop with a Sunday market

This historic industrial building dates back to 1912, when it was built to house (you guessed it) the factory of a tobacco firm. In 1998, the upper floor was transformed into a theatre that's still thriving today thanks to its lively programme of fringe shows, re-imagined classics and comedy gigs. On the ground floor, a farm shop and veggie restaurant have taken up residence – with produce grown less than 10 miles away at Five Acre Farm. On Sundays, stalls showcasing local bakers and makers fill the garden. Still, the factory hasn't totally forgotten its past: a cigarette machine by the toilets now dispenses art objects. Very Bristolian.

Raleigh Road, BS3 1TF
tobaccofactory.com

51

WIPER AND TRUE

Brewery in an industrial-park oasis

Before Michael Wiper and Al True opened their first Bristol brewery in 2015, they started out home-brewing on the kitchen hob. This spirit of experimentation is still at the heart of Wiper and True's range of interesting brews – even if the set-up is now infinitely slicker. In their new Old Market taproom – a warehouse filled with hanging plants, tonal tiles and vast windows revealing the gleaming brewery beyond – their wide-ranging roster of pale ales, lagers and stouts is served alongside boxes of dumplings from award-winning Japanese street food vendors Eatchu. Sit outside in the garden (a carpark that's been cleverly filled with greenery) and order a delectably drinkable Kaleidoscope – their signature pale ale.

Unit 11, City Business Park, Easton Road, BS5 0SP
Other location: St Werburghs
wiperandtrue.com

52

GRAIN BARGE

Food, beers and bands on a boat

Moored up in Hotwells, just across the water from Brunel's iconic SS Great Britain, this floating taproom has a below-deck bar with wrap-around windows, so you can sit back and watch the comings-and-goings of sailboats, swans and paddle-boarders around the harbour. The Grain Barge also serves up seasonal plates piled with local veg and ethically sourced seafood, including pescatarian-friendly Sunday lunches. Come summer, you might prefer to sit up top and sun yourself on the deck while sipping a North Street cider. But when night falls, it's time to head down to the hold bar, where Bristol bands regularly get the boat rocking.

Hotwell Road, BS8 4RU
grainbarge.com

53

KASK WINE

Joyfully unpretentious wine bar and shop

Whether you're a wine buff or just wish you were, KASK will make you feel welcome – then inspire you to try something new. Championing organic producers and interesting terroirs, their menu of wines available by the glass or on tap changes weekly (but always features a cheese plate specially selected to complement what's being poured). Straight-talking tasting notes will help expand your palette and, once you've found something you like, you can take a bottle of it home with you from their well-stocked shelves. Want a little more guidance? Join one of KASK's regular wine-and-cheese tasting events to be entertainingly talked through glass after glass of deliciousness.

51 North Street, BS3 1EN
kaskwine.co.uk

54

THE CANTEEN

Relaxed live music and veggie plates

There's always something happening at this beloved Stokes Croft hangout, where the multi-generational crowd of locals whiling away the day or dancing through the night makes for a welcoming atmosphere. Rock up at lunchtime for sandwiches on freshly baked focaccia or a Sunday roast, spend the afternoon trying out their range of boardgames and beers, then order some evening small plates from their seasonally changing menu – celeriac bao buns, pumpkin curry, crispy smashed potatoes with aioli and house sriracha – before tables get cleared away in time for dancing. There's free music every night (as long as you're there before 9.30pm on a Friday or Saturday) – be it a ska ensemble, a jazz jam session or a toe-tapping folk band.

80 Stokes Croft, BS1 3QY
canteenbristol.co.uk

55

LEFT HANDED GIANT

Brilliant beers brewed before your eyes

There's a theatrical feel to Left Handed Giant's brewpub, so dramatic is the sight of its facade as you cross the snaking steel structure of Castle Bridge towards the sounds of music and merriment. The impressive views continue inside, where the covered courtyard is hung with banners illustrated by in-house artist James Yeo and overlooked by three glass-fronted floors of people cheerfully carousing. And that's all before you get to the beer: known for their deep, hoppy flavours and hazy IPAs, there's always something interesting to try straight from the source here – because LHG are on a mission to reduce their emissions by minimising the distance from tank to tap.

Hawkins Lane, BS1 6EU
Other location: St Philips
lefthandedgiant.com

56

THE OLD MARKET ASSEMBLY

Live bands and club nights in an ornate venue

From raucous brass-band jazz shows to reggae weekenders, funk and soul DJ sets to queer cabaret nights, The Old Market Assembly offers up some of Bristol's best (and most eclectic) nightlife in a palatial, dome-ceilinged building that used to be a bank. But the performances don't stop there – the adjoining Wardrobe Theatre is known for its fringe studio shows and spoken word nights that capture Bristol's spirit of creative experimentation. By day, the Assembly's vibe is laidback and pub-like, with tables tucked into nooks and crannies around the ground floor and mezzanine. Wander in to grab a pint and a hand-stretched pizza – then see where the night takes you.

25 West Street, BS2 0DF
oldmarketassembly.co.uk

57

BRISTOL BEACON

Reinvigorated concert hall

Reopened after five long years of refurbishment, this iconic music venue has a new look and a new name (Bristolians having made their feelings about its previous namesake clear when they toppled Colston's statue in 2020). Its several spaces include atmospheric cellars for subterranean gigs, the ornate Victorian Lantern Hall (great for intimate folk performances) and the magnificently remodelled main auditorium, Beacon Hall. With improved acoustics, it's once again a venue fit to host global superstars (everyone from Jimi Hendrix to David Bowie has played here), but it also promises to be a beacon for Bristol-grown talent.

Trenchard Street, BS1 5AR
bristolbeacon.org

58

NUMBER 38 CLIFTON

Luxurious townhouse hotel

Perched on the edge of The Downs, a huge expanse of protected parkland high above the city, this boutique townhouse offers sleek, spotless accommodation and dramatic vistas over Bristol's rooftops. On the ground floor there's a series of snug art-adorned lounges for guests to admire the view from, while twelve serenely styled rooms provide contemporary comfort at a good range of rates. It's a bed and breakfast set-up, so you'll have to venture out for dinner – but with the many restaurants of Whiteladies Road a short walk away and littlefrench (no.15) just across The Downs, you won't be stuck for ideas.

38 Upper Belgrave Road, BS8 2XN
number38clifton.com

59

ARTIST RESIDENCE BRISTOL

Boutique bolthole in the centre of the city

This art-focused hotel has breathed new life into a Georgian townhouse and adjacent former boot factory. Its 23 rooms, which range from small-but-stylish quarters to lavish suites, have been individually designed around the building's original features – so you'll find ornate cornices framed by eclectic splashes of colour. The atmosphere is laidback and welcoming, with a downstairs 'library' (housing more art than books) for guests to hang out in, as well as a bar and restaurant that's often abuzz with Bristolians thanks to its plates of high-end comfort food and a Sunday roast menu that features four different kinds of Bloody Mary.

28 Portland Square, BS2 8SA
artistresidence.co.uk

60

MOLLIE'S

Super-stylish motel and diner

Picture a motel and the first thing that comes to mind won't be anything like Mollie's. Designed by Soho House, their teal-painted, wood-panelled rooms have everything you need (including hair straighteners) and nothing you don't. Over the road, you'll find an ode to proper American diners – leather booths, baskets of 'frickles' (fried pickles), boozy shakes and pancake stacks – that's had its own Soho style-injection. The motel-appropriate location just off the M5 may be a little outside the city, but buses to the centre are frequent. Rooms start at £70 a night and Bristol's inland surfing lake, The Wave (no.38), is just a ten-minute drive away.

Cribbs Causeway, BS10 7TL
mollies.com/Bristol

IMAGE CREDITS

An Opinionated Guide to Bristol
First edition

Published in 2024 by Hoxton Mini Press, London
Copyright © Hoxton Mini Press 2024. All rights reserved.

Text by Florence Filose
Editing by Octavia Stocker and Florence Ward
Additional design and production by Richard Mason
Proofreading by Zoë Jellicoe

With thanks to Matthew Young for initial series design.

Please note: we recommend checking the websites listed for each
entry before you visit for the latest information on price, opening times
and pre-booking requirements.

The right of Florence Filose to be identified as the creator of this Work has been
asserted under the Copyright, Designs and Patents Act 1988.

A CIP catalogue record for this book is available from the British Library.

ISBN: 978-1-914314-60-5

Printed and bound by OZGraf, Poland

Hoxton Mini Press is an environmentally conscious publisher, committed
to offsetting our carbon footprint. This book is 100 per cent carbon
compensated, with offset purchased from Stand For Trees.

Every time you order from our website, we plant a tree:
www.hoxtonminipress.com

FSC
www.fsc.org

MIX
Paper from
responsible sources
FSC® C163799

Selected opinionated guides in the series:

For more go to www.hoxtonminipress.com

INDEX